CONTEMPORARY LIVES

BEYONCÉ

SINGER, SONGWRITER, & ACTRESS

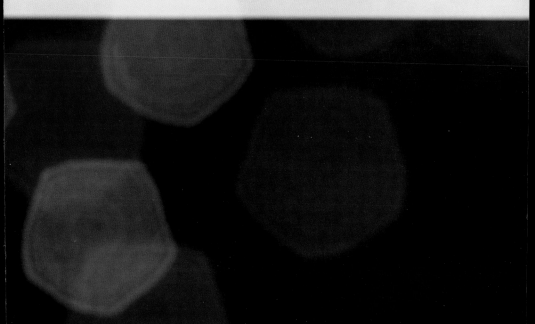

ABDO
Publishing Company

BEYONCÉ

SINGER, SONGWRITER, & ACTRESS

by Barbara Kramer

CREDITS

Published by ABDO Publishing Company, PO Box 398166,
Minneapolis, MN 55439. Copyright © 2013 by Abdo Consulting
Group, Inc. International copyrights reserved in all countries.
No part of this book may be reproduced in any form without
written permission from the publisher. The Essential Library™ is a
trademark and logo of ABDO Publishing Company.

Printed in the United States of America,
North Mankato, Minnesota
092012
012013

 THIS BOOK CONTAINS AT LEAST 10% RECYCLED MATERIALS.

Editor: Megan Anderson
Series Designer: Emily Love

Cataloging-in-Publication Data
Kramer, Barbara.
 Beyonce: singer, songwriter, & actress / Barbara Kramer.
   p. cm. -- (Contemporary lives)
Includes bibliographical references and index.
ISBN 978-1-61783-617-6
1. Beyonce, 1981- --Juvenile literature. 2. Rhythm and blues
musicians--United States--Biography--Juvenile literature. 3. Singers--
United States--Biography--Juvenile literature. 1. Title.
782.42164092--dc15
[B]

                                                              2012945990

TABLE OF CONTENTS

1   AN UNFORGETTABLE NIGHT   6

2   A RISING STAR   14

3   A DATE WITH DESTINY   24

4   A ROLLER COASTER YEAR   32

5   SURVIVING   42

6   ON HER OWN   52

7   TOGETHER AGAIN   62

8   NEW CHAPTERS   70

9   FINDING BALANCE   78

10   IN CHARGE OF HER DESTINY   86

TIMELINE   96

GET THE SCOOP   100

GLOSSARY   102

ADDITIONAL RESOURCES   104

SOURCE NOTES   106

INDEX   110

ABOUT THE AUTHOR   112

In 2011, Beyoncé became the first woman in more than 20 years to headline the Glastonbury Festival.

CHAPTER 1

An Unforgettable Night

||||||||||||||||||||||||||||||||||||

Anticipation grew as thousands of fans waited for Beyoncé to take the stage on the evening of June 26, 2011. It was the final night of the Glastonbury Festival, one of the world's largest outdoor music events. The 137,500 tickets available for that year's festival had been sold out months in advance. Now those music lovers jammed the grounds of Worthy Farm, about seven miles (11 km) outside the town of Glastonbury in Somerset, England.

Beyoncé would be bringing the three-day festival to a close on the Pyramid Stage. It marked the first time in more than 20 years a solo female performer had headlined the festival's main stage. It was rare for Beyoncé to perform at a festival—particularly before such a large audience.

"I was so scared," Beyoncé later recalled of her nervousness before the show. "I was like

THE GLASTONBURY FESTIVAL

The first Glastonbury Festival was a two-day event held in 1970. Approximately 1,500 people attended, and the price of admission included free milk from nearby Worthy Farm. By the second year, word had spread and more than 12,000 visitors attended. In 1979, the festival expanded to three days. Eventually, attendance grew and so did the entertainment. During the day, a variety of musicians perform on stages throughout the area, capped off by a headline act each evening on the Pyramid Stage. In 1998, there were more than 1,000 performances on 17 different stages. It is an almost annual festival, with a year off now and then to allow the land to recover and the cows to be outside all summer. In 2010, Glastonbury celebrated its fortieth anniversary.

The first night of the Glastonbury Festival in 2011, Irish rockers U2 headlined the Pyramid Stage, gamely performing in the rain. When the band Coldplay appeared on the main stage Saturday night, Beyoncé watched from the front row. She easily got caught up in the crowd's excitement as they sang and danced along with the music. Beyoncé said watching Coldplay perform in front of an excited and loving crowd helped calm her for her upcoming performance Sunday night.

a leaf."[1] She calmed herself with prayer, deep breathing, and positive thoughts. Then it was time to begin.

||||||||||||||||||||||||||||||||||||||||||||||||||||||||

A "GOBSMACKING" SHOW

The opening bars to Beyoncé's hit "Crazy in Love" filled the air, and the crowd erupted. Stage lights revealed a white glowing pyramid against a blue backdrop as Beyoncé rose out of the floor center stage, appearing as a silhouette in front of the pyramid as the song started. After an explosion of fireworks, the lighting changed and bathed the pyramid and stage in red.

Beyoncé had spent a lot of time deciding on the playlist for her concert at Glastonbury, as well as how she wanted the stage to look. Because she would be singing on the Pyramid Stage, the idea for the pyramid setting seemed like a natural choice. But it also had a deeper meaning. Beyoncé had recently vacationed in Egypt, and inside one of the pyramids, she felt compelled to sing the classical hymn "Ave Maria." It was such an inspiring experience, Beyoncé considered it while planning her show and was convinced a pyramid needed to be part of the stage.

Wearing a glittery gold jacket just long enough to cover her black hot pants, Beyoncé strutted across the stage in sparkly high-heeled ankle boots. Her wild, curly hair flowed freely in the breeze as she danced and sang for her frenzied fans.

One British critic called it a "gobsmacking opening," but Beyoncé was just getting started.[2] "Are you ready to be entertained?" she called out, bringing a thunderous response from the audience as she launched into her second number, "Single Ladies (Put a Ring on It)."[3] Fans sang along to hits such as "Say My Name" and pumped their fists in the air to the rhythm of "Survivor." Backed by an all-female band, Beyoncé sang about strong,

Excited festivalgoers eagerly awaited Beyoncé's performance.

independent women. "Who run the world?" she sang.[4] The answer was "Girls!" as she launched into "Run the World (Girls)," a song from her upcoming album, 4.

She closed her 90-minute show with "Halo," dedicating the song to her fans. As she sang, Beyoncé strolled down from the stage and touched the outstretched hands of her fans. On the stage, photos of people at the festival streamed across

"I'm a diva," Beyoncé said in an interview with Piers Morgan of Cable News Network (CNN) the day after her Glastonbury Festival performance.[6] For many people, the word *diva* describes women who consider themselves special and make unreasonable demands. But the word has a different meaning for Beyoncé. She says divas are graceful, talented, and brave women. When Beyoncé was young, she looked up to singers such as Patti LaBelle and Tina Turner. They were her type of divas, and she wanted to be just like them.

large screens on both sides of the pyramid. Beyoncé's team had spent three days filming and assembling the video of those smiling faces.

Returning to the stage to finish the song, Beyoncé struggled to hold back happy tears. "Thank you all for this beautiful night," she called to the roaring crowd. "I'll never forget it!"[5]

STILL SOARING

Two hours later, Beyoncé sat down with Lauren Laverne and Jo Whiley for an interview with the British Broadcasting Corporation (BBC). She was dressed casually in light blue jeans and a white top. She had replaced her high-heeled boots with wellies, the same knee-high rubber boots many fans wore during the first two days of the festival as rain turned the grounds into a muddy swamp. Beyoncé joked hers didn't look right because they were so squeaky-clean. "I definitely need some mud!" she exclaimed.[7]

Her sparkly gold jacket was gone, but the excitement of the evening was not. "I will never, ever, ever, ever, ever forget this . . . this night," Beyoncé said.[8]

Playing for the large crowd at Glastonbury had been a risk, but Beyoncé believed in pushing herself to new limits. "Right now, this part of my life is all about embracing change and going to the next level, taking risks and showing my bravery," she said.[9]

||||||||||

Beyoncé discovered her musical talent at an early age.

CHAPTER 2

A Rising Star

||||||||||||||||||||||||||||||||||||||||||||||||||||||||||||||||||||||||||||||||

Beyoncé Giselle Knowles was born in Houston, Texas, on September 4, 1981. She was the oldest daughter of Mathew and Tina Knowles. Her sister, Solange, was born on June 24, 1986.

When Beyoncé was growing up, there was always music in the Knowles home. Although she came from a musical family, her parents never imagined she would one day become a performer because she was such a shy child. "She'd

Beyoncé's name was the result of an agreement between her parents, who decided each of them could choose a name. Mathew picked Giselle, while Tina chose Beyoncé, which was her maiden name. Although Beyoncé now embraces her easily identifiable name, many of her classmates teased her because they didn't know how to pronounce it correctly. But when Beyoncé became famous, reporters offered a little assistance: her name rhymes with fiancée.

come into a room and just want to be invisible," her mother, Tina, recalls.[1]

When Beyoncé was seven, her mother enrolled her in dance classes. Beyoncé's teacher soon realized her student had something special, encouraging Beyoncé to sing as well as dance and convincing her to enter a local talent show.

For the talent show, Beyoncé planned to sing John Lennon's "Imagine," a song about the dream of a world where people live in peace. Her dad thought she needed to understand the meaning of the song, so three days before the show he wrote down the lyrics and discussed them with her. When it was time to perform, Beyoncé was scared, but she felt calm once the music started. "I

Mathew and Tina Knowles have supported and encouraged their daughter's music career.

don't know what happened. I just . . . changed," she said.[2] She got a standing ovation and won the competition.

TAKING THE STAGE

After that first performance, Beyoncé sang wherever she could find an audience that would listen. She began taking voice lessons, singing in the church choir, and entering more talent shows. The talent shows were more like beauty contests, and while Beyoncé enjoyed performing, she did not like getting dressed up. However, she realized it was part of the competition, and she liked winning trophies. Before long, she had accumulated more than 30 of them.

In 1990, when Beyoncé was nine, her parents took her to the People's Workshop in Houston. That nonprofit organization promoted local

ROLE MODELS

Beyoncé is often criticized for working too hard, and she admits she's been a perfectionist ever since she was a kid. It is a trait Beyoncé probably inherited from her parents. Mathew was a leading salesperson of medical equipment at Xerox, including magnetic resonance imaging (MRI) and computed tomography (CT)–scan machinery. Tina owned a successful hair salon in Houston. Beyoncé saw her mother work 13-hour days styling hair and managing the business. She had calluses on her fingers and swollen feet, but she never complained. "My parents and the drive they have, it's kind of worn off on me," Beyoncé said.[3]

talent and gave her an opportunity to sing for talent scouts in the area. Beyoncé's talent caught the attention of two women, who invited her to audition for an all-girl rhythm and blues (R&B) group they were putting together.

|||||||||||||||||||||||||||||||||||||||||||||||||||||||

GIRL'S TYME

Beyoncé competed against more than 50 girls auditioning for a spot in the group, which became known as Girl's Tyme. Beyoncé made the cut and met LaTavia Roberson, a dancer with the group. Although Beyoncé had been a solo performer, she enjoyed being part of a group, working on songs and dance moves together and sharing the excitement of being on stage.

The group was constantly changing as a new rotation of girls replaced members who left. Eventually, more than 100 girls performed with Girl's Tyme, but LaTavia and Beyoncé stayed with the group. In 1991, a new member, Kelly Rowland, joined the group after relocating to Houston from Atlanta, Georgia.

Kelly's mother, Doris, was a single parent who worked as a live-in nanny. They moved often, and she wanted a more stable life for her daughter. Kelly, Beyoncé, and the other girls from Girl's Tyme spent a lot of time together rehearsing, usually at Beyoncé's house. Because Kelly spent so much time at the Knowles home already, Doris and Beyoncé's parents decided Kelly would come and stay with them.

Although Kelly and Beyoncé were great friends, being roommates was an adjustment. Beyoncé had to learn to share everything—closet space, the phone, and even her parents.

||||||||||||||||||||||||||||||||||||||||||||||||||||

A NEW HOME ||||||||||||||||||||||||||||||||||||||||||||||||||||||||||||||||||||||||||||||||||||||||||||||||||||

Kelly knew it was hard for her mother to let her move in with the Knowles family, but she understood that Doris wanted what was best for her. Later, Beyoncé's parents, Mathew and Tina, were criticized in the press for taking Kelly away from her mother, but Tina told *Entertainment Weekly*, "Kelly's mom had a key to our house and to our car. Most weekends she stayed with us. She has been a part of Kelly's life every day."[4]

Beyoncé started out performing for small audiences in the Houston area.

REACHING FOR STARDOM

Girl's Tyme reached a national audience in 1992, when the group appeared on the popular television talent competition *Star Search*. The six group members were all between the ages of 11 and 12, and they had practiced and rehearsed for months in preparation for the show in Los Angeles, California. Their opponent was rock band Skeleton Crew, a previous *Star Search* winner back to defend its title.

Girl's Tyme took the stage wearing shorts, brightly colored satin jackets, and white boots. After a rapping LaTavia opened for the group, Beyoncé performed the vocals while the rest of the group energetically danced their hip-hop routine. A panel of judges scored both acts at the end of the show. Skeleton Crew was awarded four stars, the highest possible score, while Girl's Tyme received three stars.

TRYING HARDER

The show *Star Search*, hosted by Ed McMahon, was televised from 1983 to 1995. Contestants competed in one of four categories—singing, dancing, modeling, and stand-up comedy. Many young talents got their first big break on the competition series. Other contestants, such as Justin Timberlake and Britney Spears, lost on the show but later went on to become famous. One producer even told Mathew Knowles that losers on the show were more likely to become successful because they were determined to reorganize and work harder to make it in the business.

The young Girl's Tyme members managed to hold it together as the winner was announced and the camera zoomed in for a close-up of the group. But as soon as the show cut to a commercial, the disappointed girls ran backstage and cried.

||||||||||||

Clockwise from left: LeToya, Beyoncé, LaTavia, and Kelly waited six years before they landed a recording contract.

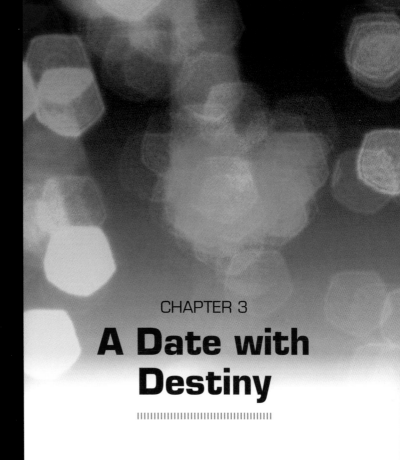

CHAPTER 3

A Date with Destiny

||||||||||||||||||||||||||||||||||||||||||||

Mathew Knowles took Kelly and Beyoncé to Disneyland in nearby Anaheim, California, hoping it would cheer them up following their *Star Search* loss. It did, but when they returned to Houston, Beyoncé watched the performance on television and cried again. She was ready to quit, but her dad encouraged her to focus on how she felt while she was performing.

The loss on *Star Search* was a huge setback for Girl's Tyme, but the group watched the tape from the performance repeatedly and examined the mistakes the girls had made. Beyoncé, Kelly, LaTavia, and LeToya agreed to work harder to improve, learning new songs and dance routines and also exercising as they practiced. The four girls jogged while singing to build their endurance so they wouldn't run out of breath during their dance routines. They also spent time studying the dance moves and performances of famous groups such as the Supremes and the Jackson 5.

Beyoncé realized she liked it too much to stop after one disappointment.

When Beyoncé's parents saw she was serious about pursuing her passion for music, Mathew stepped in to support her dream. Mathew created a new group with Beyoncé, Kelly, LaTavia, and LeToya Luckett, a girl Beyoncé knew from school, who joined the group in 1993.

|||||||||||||||||||||||||||||||||||||||||||||||||||||||||

THE QUEST FOR A RECORDING CONTRACT

At first, the new group referred to themselves as Somethin' Fresh, but they went through several names, including Cliché and The Dolls. They ultimately settled on Destiny, which Tina suggested after reading it in the Bible.

Under Mathew's direction, the girls took voice lessons and practiced for hours each day. Beyoncé, Kelly, LaTavia, and LeToya worked with a choreographer to perfect their dance routines, and a media coach trained them for interviews and public appearances.

To keep the group in the public eye, Mathew scheduled at least one appearance each week and twice per week during the summer. They sang at churches, grocery store openings, fashion shows, and amusement parks. Soon Destiny became well-known around the Houston area.

Meanwhile, Tina encouraged the girls to maintain balance in their lives. Tina told Beyoncé and Kelly to continue having fun like other girls their age, going to slumber parties and hanging out with friends.

A BUSINESS MODEL

Although Mathew Knowles had no experience with the music industry, he said his work as a salesperson had prepared him for building relationships and making business decisions. Mathew patterned his business, Music World Entertainment, and style after Berry Gordy Jr., the founder of Motown Records. Gordy worked with artists such as the Supremes, the Jackson 5, and Stevie Wonder. Mathew liked that Gordy not only took charge of all aspects of producing albums, but also taught his performers to act like stars in how they walked, dressed, and talked during interviews. "He had real artist development. And his artists were glamorous," Mathew said. "That's really what the music world is all about."[1]

Beyoncé attended the private Saint Mary's Elementary School, but enrolled in a public school when she started eighth grade. Beyoncé started high school in 1995, but left after the first semester to focus on her career. After that, she was tutored.

A BAD AUDITION

In 1995, Mathew successfully arranged for the group to audition for Teresa LaBarbera Whites from Columbia Records. The day before the audition, he instructed the girls not to go swimming because they would get stuffed up, but they didn't listen, and the next day they were all congested. Mathew was so upset he stopped them in the middle of their performance and made them start over. Despite the bad performance, Whites seemed impressed with Destiny's discipline and Mathew's guidance.

The group also attracted the attention of songwriter and producer Daryl Simmons from Silent Partner Productions, who had connections with Elektra Records and offered Destiny a recording contract. Columbia Records also expressed interest in the group.

||||||||||||||||||||||||||||||||||||||||||||||||||||||||

AWAY FROM HOME

Mathew decided to sign with Silent Partner Productions, and Destiny moved to Atlanta, Georgia, where the company was headquartered. LaTavia's mother accompanied the four girls as a chaperone. They all lived together in the basement of the house of Simmons's assistant. Each morning, the girls met with their tutor for schooling, and the rest of the day was spent in the recording studio.

> "We were nice ladies. I mean, I'm not sayin' that we were perfect teenagers. But, we were raised well and, honestly, we were too busy tryin' to be superstars. We didn't even have time to think about it, honestly."[3]
>
> —*BEYONCÉ*

Destiny's dream, however, came to an end a few months later when the company dropped them without releasing a single recording. "We felt like our life was over," Beyoncé recalled.[2]

There were also problems in the Knowles home. Mathew had quit his high-paying sales job at Xerox to manage Destiny full time. Tina's hair salon was doing well, but the family was used to living on two incomes. They were forced to sell their house and move into a smaller home. The financial problems caused so much strain and tension in Tina and Mathew's marriage they decided to separate in 1996.

Beyoncé, Solange, and Kelly moved into a small apartment with Tina. Fortunately, the separation lasted only a few months and the family reunited.

Early on, Destiny's Child dreamed of future success.

Meanwhile, Mathew continued pursuing a recording contract. He contacted Whites at Columbia Records, who flew them to New York City for another audition in 1996. Destiny returned to Houston unsure if they had convinced the record company.

Two weeks later, they found out they had landed the recording contract. "That was our turning point and we all knew it," Beyoncé said.[4]

|||||||||||

Destiny's Child's first album eventually sold 3 million copies worldwide.

CHAPTER 4

A Roller Coaster Year

||||||||||||||||||||||||||||||||||||||||||||||||||||||||||||||||||||||||||||||||

Destiny's first release with Columbia Records was in 1997, when the group recorded the song "Killing Time" for the movie soundtrack to *Men in Black*. The girls also took another look at the name of their group. Mathew did some research and discovered there were several groups named Destiny. So they added *Child*, becoming Destiny's Child.

Destiny's Child actually recorded two versions of "No, No, No." The first version of the song was slow, and the group returned to the studio to do a remix with rapper Wyclef Jean. Jean had risen to fame as a member of the rap group the Fugees. One day, as Beyoncé was recording her vocals, Jean instructed her to hurry because studio time is expensive and the album was already running over budget. Joking around, Beyoncé started singing the lyrics really fast. But Jean liked it so much they recorded the song that way. Both versions of "No, No, No" are featured on the album, but the more upbeat, remixed version became a huge hit.

In November 1997, when Beyoncé was 16, they released "No, No, No," their first single from their upcoming first album, *Destiny's Child*. Beyoncé and Rowland were picking up Solange after school the first time they heard the song on the radio. When they heard it playing, they cranked up the volume, got out of the car, and started dancing.

Their self-titled album, *Destiny's Child*, was released in February 1998. Although sales were lukewarm at first, it eventually went platinum. Still, the members of Destiny's Child were not satisfied. They knew they could do better.

SECOND ALBUM

For their second effort, the performers wanted to be more involved with the creative process. "A lot of artists who inspire us told us we needed to write and produce," Beyoncé said.[1] She took on more of that role for their next album, *The Writing's on the Wall.*

"Bills, Bills, Bills" was the first single from the album released in May 1999. It quickly climbed the *Billboard* singles chart, where it spent nine weeks at Number 1.

STYLING |||||||||||||||||||||||||||||||||||||||||||||||||||||||||||||||||||||||||||||||||||||||||||

For Destiny's Child's first photo shoot, Columbia provided a team to style the singers' hair, makeup, and clothes. But the group was unhappy with the result because the clothes didn't reflect their fashion tastes. Tina, who had been in charge of their style before their recording contract, took over again while Destiny's Child was in Jamaica filming for Music Television's (MTV) Spring Break. The costumes were a success, particularly with the girls, who felt they matched their personalities. After that, Tina became the group's primary stylist. "She knows our strengths and weaknesses and always makes us look great," Rowland said.[2]

When Beyoncé was 15, her mother took her and the other girls from Destiny's Child to a Janet Jackson concert. "The others were like, 'That was great,'" Tina Knowles recalled, "but Beyoncé was already pulling it apart, trying to figure out what made it good. She said, 'One day I want to have a concert like that.'"[3]

The album was released in July, and the next months were hectic while Destiny's Child promoted it. There were interviews and appearances, and that fall, Destiny's Child went on tour with another popular female group, TLC.

DOWNHILL RIDE

As the group's popularity grew, cracks were appearing within Destiny's Child. For more than a year, there had been conflicts among the four group members, who tried working through their problems and even visited with their pastor for counseling. Beyoncé thought everything was fine, but in December 1999, Roberson and Luckett each sent Mathew a letter dissolving their management agreement with him and requesting their own manager. The request was something Beyoncé said

Mathew and the group considered, but realized would never work. Beyoncé said the conflict within the group had been brewing for a while, saying,

> When you're a group, then you have to be a group. You can't be two and two. Anyone who ever was around us would notice that two would be here, two would be there.[4]

By January 2000, Roberson and Luckett were no longer members of Destiny's Child. Critics and the media turned on Beyoncé, blaming her for the problems within the group. Beyoncé was so depressed she stayed in her room for a short period, but eventually she knew she had to move forward. Beyoncé said of dealing with the group's turmoil: "When unexpected things happen that you have little or no control over, you have to sink or you swim and sinking wasn't part of the program."[5]

Destiny's Child now needed to find two replacements, and time was of the essence. The group was preparing to shoot a music video for its single "Say My Name." Because the song was already playing on the radio, it needed an accompanying music video to help promote it.

UNFAIR JUDGMENT

Utilizing Destiny's Child's connections in the industry, they found two new members, Michelle Williams and Farrah Franklin. Franklin was a dancer in the Destiny's Child music video for "Bills, Bills, Bills," and Williams had met them on tour while she was a backup singer for R&B artist Monica.

With only two weeks to prepare for the video, Beyoncé, Rowland, Williams, and Franklin worked 12-hour days perfecting their routines. They also added more dancers in hopes that the group changes wouldn't be as noticeable with more people in the music video when it debuted in February 2000.

Internal conflict forced the group to find two new members, Franklin and Williams.

But if fans were disappointed by the behind-the-scenes changes to Destiny's Child, it didn't impact sales. "Say My Name" became the album's second Number 1 single, staying at the top of the charts for three weeks, and *The Writing's on the Wall* went multiplatinum.

On March 15, 2000, Roberson and Luckett filed a lawsuit against Mathew. They accused him of favoring Beyoncé and Rowland and claimed that he was too controlling. The lawsuit was later settled out of court.

ANOTHER HILL TO CLIMB

The newly configured Destiny's Child's success continued at a hectic pace. The performers' first live performance was at the NBA All-Star weekend. The group then made its television debut on the Soul Train Music Awards, and in April, they appeared on VH1's *Divas 2000: A Tribute to Diana Ross*. Then they embarked on a European tour.

However, Franklin missed several promotional appearances, and then informed the group she would not be joining them for an upcoming Australian tour. Beyoncé, Rowland, and Williams scrambled to change the vocals and dance routines so they were suitable for a trio.

In July 2000, Destiny's Child decided to continue on as a trio. Destiny's Child began touring

OVERCOMING CONFLICTS ||||||||||||||||||||||||||||||||||||||||||||||||||||||||||||||

Many music groups have disbanded after experiencing similar turmoil as Destiny's Child, including struggles for control and member changes. Beyoncé was just happy fans stuck with the group, which she believes was because the members still managed to put on a good performance. "When we get up on the stage and we sing and perform, that's the thing that really matters," she noted.[7]

Destiny's Child moved forward as a trio with Rowland, *left*, Beyoncé, *center*, and Williams, *right*.

with pop star Christina Aguilera until September, then headed into the recording studio. They took home *Billboard*'s Artist of the Year Award in December 2000. The honors continued into 2001, when they won two Grammys for "Say My Name," Best R&B Group Performance and Best R&B Song. Beyoncé was optimistic about Destiny's Child, saying, "The great thing about the roller coaster we're on is that we're going up, up, up."[8]

Beyoncé took on a creative role as cowriter for Destiny's Child's second album.

CHAPTER 5

Surviving

||||||||||||||||||||||||||||||||||||||||||||||||||||||

One of Destiny's Child's first hit singles, "Bills, Bills, Bills," is about a guy who took advantage of a girl by running up charges on her credit card. Another hit from the album *The Writing's on the Wall,* "Say My Name," is about a woman who suspects her man is cheating. The subjects of those songs caused some to speculate if Destiny's Child was really against men. The group wasn't against men, but Beyoncé said they did have a message for women: no one deserves to be treated poorly in a relationship.

Beyoncé continued that spirit of self-sufficient women able to make it on their own by writing "Independent Women (Part 1)." The song was released on the *Charlie's Angels* soundtrack. The movie starred Drew Barrymore, Lucy Liu, and Cameron Diaz and premiered in October 2000. "Independent Women (Part 1)" was the first single released from the film's soundtrack and spent 11 weeks in the Number 1 spot on *Billboard's* Hot 100.

The song was also included on *Survivor,* the third album recorded by Destiny's Child. The album sold 663,000 copies following its May 2001 release, setting a new record for

BECOMING AN INDEPENDENT WOMAN ||||||||||||

Following the success of the song "Independent Women (Part 1)," a reporter asked Beyoncé what it meant to be an independent woman. Beyoncé replied, "Someone who works really hard. Someone with strength, goals, respect for herself. She knows what she wants and works hard to achieve whatever that is."[1] The reporter then asked if Beyoncé was that type of woman, to which Beyoncé responded, "I'm working on it!"[2]

Beyoncé says the inspiration for another song from *Survivor*, "Bootylicious," came from her own personal struggle with weight. "I like to eat and that's a problem in this industry," she said.[3] Beyoncé disliked having to worry about her weight all the time, so she wrote the song to let girls know it was okay to be something other than super thin. Rapper Snoop Dogg first coined the term *bootylicious* in 1992, and it is used as an adjective describing a sexually attractive woman. Due to the popularity of the Destiny's Child song, *bootylicious* was added to the Oxford Dictionary of English in 2004.

first-week sales by a female group. For Columbia Records, it generated the biggest opening week in the record company's history.

Beyoncé cowrote most of the songs for the album, which focus on people surviving various trials. The album's title song told the group's personal account of reaching the top of the music industry despite obstacles along the way. The song "Story of Beauty" was inspired by a fan who wrote the group about her personal story of being molested by a stepfather.

Beyoncé was also coproducer of the album, and group members Williams and Rowland were thrilled with the result. Rowland said, "A great thing is Beyoncé is a writer and a producer. She will open up the doors to younger writers and producers that are females."[4] Williams said, "She brought out the best in us because she knows us. She knew what we could do, and she made sure that we did it."[5]

Destiny's Child was nominated for three Grammys in February 2002, and the group won for Best R&B Vocal Performance by a Duo or Group for "Survivor." *Survivor* influenced many Destiny's Child fans, giving some the courage to escape bad relationships. Recovering alcoholics made "Survivor" their theme song. Beyoncé wanted to do more to help. The Knowles family and Rowland donated part of their record sale earnings to build a youth center in Houston where teenagers could go rather than spending time on the street.

NEW DIRECTIONS

As Beyoncé grew as a performer, writer, and producer, she also crossed over into acting in May 2001. She portrayed the title role in the MTV movie *Carmen: A Hip Hopera,* opposite actor Mekhi

The Destiny's Child trio won the 2002 Grammy for Best R&B Vocal Performance for "Survivor."

Phifer, in an update of a classic nineteenth-century opera. The character of Carmen was a deceitful woman, the complete opposite of Beyoncé's personality, which provided her with a good opportunity to showcase her acting abilities.

The movie also allowed her to grow personally as well. Throughout Beyoncé's music career, she had relied on her family and the other members of Destiny's Child. But *Carmen* was filmed in Los Angeles, California, meaning she was on her own for the first time. Of the filming experience Beyoncé said,

> *"It doesn't seem like a big thing, but I was away from home, away from everything. Besides a new job, I had to make friends in a new city. I call it my college."*[6]

FOXXY CLEOPATRA

In November 2001, Destiny's Child released its Christmas album, *8 Days of Christmas*. The members also announced the group would be taking a break in order for Beyoncé, Rowland, and Williams to pursue other interests. The three of them were working on solo albums, and Beyoncé was filming another movie, *Austin Powers in Goldmember.*

Austin Powers in Goldmember was the third installment in a popular spy comedy movie series starring comedian Mike Meyers. The films parodied other popular spy movies, such as the James Bond films. Beyoncé portrayed Foxxy Cleopatra, a spy

Austin Powers in Goldmember producer John Lyons was confident Beyoncé was the right choice for the part of Foxxy Cleopatra from the beginning. Lyons had discovered her when he saw the MTV hip-hop version of *Carmen*. "She lit up every frame of that project and that was just her first acting role," Lyons noted.[8] His recommendation secured her an audition even as director Jay Roach looked at more experienced actresses. Beyoncé didn't think she did a very good job at the audition, but she got a callback. She nailed the second audition by showing up with attitude and wearing a 1970s-style jumpsuit and a big curly wig.

posing as the lead singer of a women's trio at a roller disco in the 1970s.

Beyoncé admitted she was nervous about working with Meyers, but he had nothing but praise for her. He described her as "a joy to work with and extremely silly."[7]

|||||||||||||||||||||||||||||||||||||||||||||||||||||||||

FINDING A MATCH

Others on the *Goldmember* set were occupied with finding a boyfriend for Beyoncé, who was a little embarrassed because she didn't want to come off

Beyoncé made the transition to the big screen with *Goldmember*.

as desperate. Beyoncé had dated a guy throughout high school, but they had less time to spend together while she began focusing more on her career, leading to their breakup.

Traveling also made starting new relationships difficult because Beyoncé was never in the same place for long. "Unless they're a dancer on the road with us, or a DJ or something. It's just very difficult," she said.[9]

Beyoncé performed "Hey Goldmember," the theme song for the *Austin Powers in Goldmember* movie soundtrack with her younger sister, Solange. This wasn't the first time the two had worked together. When Solange first decided she wanted to be a performer, Mathew told her she should go on tour to learn more about the business. Solange followed his advice and toured with Destiny's Child as a dancer. She is also a songwriter, and her first album, *Solo Star,* was released in 2003. Solange had a son, Daniel, on October 18, 2004. Beyoncé has admitted she is protective of Solange, telling *Essence* magazine: "Solange is the one person I will fight for. Don't talk about my sister; don't play with me about my sister. If you do, you'll see another side of me."[11]

Critics were not impressed with *Goldmember*, but Beyoncé was praised for her role. Veteran movie critic Roger Ebert wanted to see more of her but said, "Alas, the movie doesn't do much with her except assign her to look extremely good while standing next to Austin."[10]

The movie grossed $71.5 million in its opening weekend in July 2002, setting a new record for the highest opening for a comedy ever. That was a huge audience for Beyoncé's first appearance in a major motion picture.

||||||||||||

Destiny's Child won the
2002 American Music
Award for Favorite Pop/
Rock Album for *Survivor*.

CHAPTER 6

On Her Own

||||||||||||||||||||||||||||||||||||||||||||||||||||||||||||||||||||||||||||||||||||||

W hile Beyoncé was filming *Goldmember,* she learned former Destiny's Child members Luckett and Roberson had filed another lawsuit in March 2002. The basis for the lawsuit concerned lyrics from the song "Survivor," which included the lines: "You thought I wouldn't sell without you/ Sold nine million."[1] Luckett and Roberson argued the lyrics were referring to them and the success Destiny's Child was enjoying after they left the group. The lines, they argued, violated their agreement from the previous lawsuit, which prohibited either party from making comments against the other.

Beyoncé, however, argued the song was about all the people who doubted Destiny's Child would succeed, including the record company that first signed them and then dropped them shortly after. The lawsuit was eventually settled out of court.

DOWN TIME

Beyoncé's solo album was due out in the fall of 2002, but she made a surprising decision to postpone its debut until 2003. Then Beyoncé took some time off during the summer of 2002, triggering media reports she was having a

THE STORY OF DESTINY'S CHILD

In the spring of 2002, Beyoncé, Rowland, and Williams released their book, *Soul Survivors: The Official Autobiography of Destiny's Child.* They wrote about experiences including their childhoods, struggles, rise to fame, and problems among the group members as they started enjoying success. They also wrote about drawing strength from their faith in God and using it to rise above challenges along the way.

breakdown. But Beyoncé said those reports were exaggerated—she was just tired. She had been working almost nonstop since her first recording contract, and it had taken its toll. "You lose touch with who you are," she said. "When you work so much like we did, it's just too much."[2]

Beyoncé spent that time off in Miami, Florida, enjoying the beach and painting, a hobby she began when she was working on *Austin Powers in Goldmember*. She also worked on her music, writing and recording 43 songs. Beyoncé joked many of them weren't tracks anyone would want to hear, but others would eventually make their way onto her first solo album.

||||||||||||||||||||||||||||||||||||||||||||||||||||||||||

BACK AT WORK

That fall, Beyoncé filmed another movie, *The Fighting Temptations*, starring opposite Oscar-winning actor Cuba Gooding Jr. She played Lilly, a single mother in a small town who is snubbed by the other women in the church choir. Beyoncé was drawn to the movie's music, as well as the character. "I liked the idea of playing someone

Beyoncé combined her vocal and acting skills again in *The Fighting Temptations*.

who valued her faith but didn't have a perfect life," she said.[3]

Once filming wrapped, Beyoncé went back to work on her album, *Dangerously in Love*, which she cowrote and coproduced. In May 2003, the first single from the album, "Crazy in Love," was released. The single featured rapper Jay-Z, and rumors began swirling that the two were romantically involved.

The media observed that the two were an unlikely couple. Jay-Z is 11 years older than Beyoncé. He also had a bad-boy reputation and was known to be a playboy. That did not seem to jibe with Beyoncé's wholesome image. On the other hand, they were both hardworking and had much in common, including their musical abilities and interest in the music business.

NO COMMENT

Beyoncé chose not to answer whenever anyone inquired about her relationship with Jay-Z. She had lived most of her life in the limelight, but she felt

THE RIGHT TOUCH

Beyoncé struggled with her recording of "Crazy in Love." One night while working late and still unsatisfied with the song, she came up with the idea to include a rapper in the song. Beyoncé had collaborated with rapper Jay-Z on one of his singles, "03 Bonnie & Clyde" in 2002. She contacted him and, even though it was the middle of the night, he came into the studio. After listening to the song, Jay-Z then recorded his rap without writing anything down. Beyoncé had seen Jay-Z perform an impromptu rap many times before, and this time it provided just the spirit the song was missing. "He added a lot to the energy of it," Beyoncé said.[4]

Jay-Z was born Shawn Corey Carter on December 4, 1969, in Brooklyn, New York. He is a rapper, songwriter, producer, and entrepreneur and one of the most successful hip-hop artists in the United States. Jay-Z grew up and started rapping in Brooklyn's Marcy housing projects, one of the most dangerous neighborhoods in the United States during the 1980s. In 1995, Jay-Z created an independent record label, Roc-A-Fella Records, with friends Damon Dash and Kareem Biggs. He made his debut with his album *Reasonable Doubt*, released in 1996. With 11 studio albums as of June 2012, Jay-Z has sold more than 50 million records worldwide. He also founded Rocawear, an urban clothing line, in 1999 and is part-owner of the Brooklyn Nets NBA team. Jay-Z was worth an estimated $450 million as of 2011.

some things should be kept private. They remained fiercely private, even as they were seen in public together more and more. "It's important to protect certain things. I don't want my relationship to be what people talk about," Beyoncé said.[5] Jay-Z also told *People* magazine, "We don't play with our relationship."[6]

However, it appeared Beyoncé did have love on her mind. *Dangerously in Love* includes songs about various relationship stages, such as meeting someone, saying "I love you" for the first time, and experiencing disappointment after being let down by someone in a relationship.

BY HERSELF

Dangerously in Love was released in July 2003, debuting at Number 1 on the *Billboard* 200. Then Beyoncé had to travel extensively to promote it, which she later admitted was difficult without the other members of Destiny's Child. Rowland had been with Beyoncé since she was nine years old, singing, performing, and doing interviews. But now Beyoncé was doing these things on her own:

> *But it's a necessary challenge because I'm an adult. We're all adults now, and we need to learn*

SOLO ACTS

While Beyoncé was acting and working on her first solo album, the other members of Destiny's Child were pursuing solo opportunities as well. In 2002, Rowland had a recurring role on the ABC comedy series *The Hughleys*. Rowland released a solo R&B album, *Simply Deep*, in 2002, and had a starring role in the 2003 horror movie *Freddie vs. Jason*. Williams also released a solo album, *Heart to Yours*, which debuted at Number 2 on *Billboard's* gospel chart.

Beyoncé and Jay-Z performed "Crazy in Love" on MTV's *Total Request Live*.

things about ourselves, and sometimes you can't do that unless you're by yourself.[7]

Beyoncé's solo efforts came to fruition on February 8, 2004, when she took home five awards on Grammy night. That night, Beyoncé also joined legendary singer-performer Prince to perform a medley of his songs for the show's opening number and later performed the title song from *Dangerously in Love*.

In March 2004, Beyoncé joined singer Alicia Keyes and rapper Missy Elliot for their five-week Ladies First tour. The tour was immensely successful, grossing $20 million for 27 performances. By April, Beyoncé was back in the studio again working on what would be the final act for Destiny's Child.

||||||||||

Destiny's Child reunited in Japan to kick off their last tour together in 2005.

CHAPTER 7

Together Again

||||||||||||||||||||||||||||||||||||||||||||||||||||||||||||||||||||||||||||||||||||||||

A s promised, Destiny's Child reunited for another album in 2004. But Beyoncé, Rowland, and Williams knew before work even began it would be their last, inspiring its title: *Destiny Fulfilled*. The album was released on November 16, 2004, debuting at Number 2 on the *Billboard* 200.

Destiny's Child kicked off its tour, Destiny Fulfilled . . . And Loving It, in Japan on April 9, 2005. About two months later, while performing a show in Barcelona, Spain, Destiny's Child announced it would be the group's last tour.

The news, Beyoncé said, did not mean they would never perform together again, and there was always the possibility they would appear on each other's albums or tours. "We love each other, and we love singing together. This is not one of those situations where there's a bad ending because something crazy happened," Beyoncé said.[1]

When the tour ended in Vancouver, Canada, on September 10, 2005, it was an emotional night. Rowland was the first to cry during her solo, and all three women were emotional by the end of the show.

"[Beyoncé] has not only influenced pop culture with her hit songs and her signature dance moves, but has inspired women everywhere with her unique style, business savvy and dedication to charitable causes."[2]

—BILL WERDE, BILLBOARD EDITORIAL DIRECTOR

HOUSE OF DERÉON

In 2005, Beyoncé teamed up with her mother to create a clothing line called the House of Deréon. The line was named for Beyoncé's grandmother, Agnez Deréon, who was a seamstress and enjoyed designing clothes. Its tagline is "Couture, Kick, Soul." Tina brings the couture, Beyoncé adds the kick, and her grandmother provides the soul. Deréon died in 1984, but Beyoncé has said she is with them in spirit.

MOVING FORWARD

On October 25, 2005, Destiny's Child released one final album, simply called *#1's*, a compilation of the group's greatest hits plus three new tracks. Beyoncé wrote one of the songs, "Check on It," for the soundtrack for her upcoming movie, *The Pink Panther*, which was based on the 1964 version.

The new film featured Beyoncé, actor Kevin Kline, and comedian Steve Martin as bumbling Inspector Clouseau. Beyoncé starred as pop star Xania. But a bigger film opportunity was on the horizon. When *The Pink Panther* was released in February 2006, Beyoncé was already at work filming her next movie, *Dreamgirls*.

Beyoncé costarred in *Dreamgirls* with Jennifer Hudson, *center,* and Anika Noni Rose, *right.*

A DREAM ROLE

Based on the successful Broadway musical, *Dreamgirls* is about the Dreamettes, a fictional R&B girl group from the 1960s. Beyoncé starred as lead singer Deena Jones. The film was inspired by the era's famous girl group, Diana Ross and the Supremes. Beyoncé had admired Ross since she was a child and was convinced she was born to play Deena. The movie, released on December 15, 2006, marked Beyoncé's first major acting role. It earned her a 2007 Golden Globe award nomination for Best Actress in a Motion Picture–Comedy or Musical.

Beyoncé said filming *Dreamgirls* was a vacation compared to recording and promoting an album. "Just being in one place for six months was a break for me. It's different from being on tour and traveling non-stop," she said.[3] Beyoncé tried taking a real vacation after filming, but she had too many songs running through her head. She was so anxious, she began working on her next album without telling her dad or anyone at her record label. This strategy gave her freedom from deadlines.

Beyoncé decided to try something she had learned from observing Jay-Z. Rather than using

MEETING AN IDOL

Beyoncé was excited to play the character loosely based on singer Diana Ross in the movie *Dreamgirls,* but she was also nervous about it. Then she ran into Ross at a pre-Grammy party in Los Angeles. Beyoncé recalled:

"I had pictures of her all over my movie trailer, and there she was, right in front of me. I was terrified. Then she tapped me on the shoulder and told me she was happy I was doing Dreamgirls. I thought I would pass out."[4]

just one studio, she had different producers working in three different rooms at once, resulting in great creative energy as the producers fed off each other. Beyoncé and her producers worked long hours to complete the album in only three weeks. The album, *B'Day*, was released internationally on September 4, 2006, Beyoncé's twenty-fifth birthday.

While planning her next tour, Beyoncé decided she wanted an all-female band performing with her, and women flew in from all over the world to

Beyoncé performs at Madison Square Garden during The Beyoncé Experience tour in August 2007.

audition. Beyoncé ended up with 10 musicians for her band, called Suga Mamas.

On April 10, 2007, Beyoncé kicked off The Beyoncé Experience tour to promote her new album. During the US leg of the tour, she teamed up with the charity Feeding America to hold food drives at some concerts. Fans brought nonperishable food items, which were donated to local food banks around the country. The tour concluded in Las Vegas, Nevada, on December 30, 2007. Soon Beyoncé would have another surprise for her fans.

||||||||||

Beyoncé and Jay-Z married in a secret wedding on April 4, 2008.

CHAPTER 8

New Chapters

lthough Beyoncé and Jay-Z had been together for over five years, they never made any public statements about their relationship. So it was no surprise that their wedding was top secret. Beyoncé and Jay-Z were married April 4, 2008, in a private ceremony at Jay-Z's New York City penthouse.

The couple and about 40 guests, including family and close friends, reportedly danced until 5 a.m. The next day, Jay-Z was performing with singer Mary J. Blige, who leaked the news of the wedding by wishing the couple well onstage: "Congratulations to my man Jay-Z and my girl B."[1]

"What Jay and I have is real. It's not about interviews or getting the right photo op. It's real."[2]

—BEYONCÉ

A CHALLENGING ROLE

Beyoncé was also right back at work filming her latest movie, *Cadillac Records*, in Louisiana. The story was based on the legendary Chicago blues record label Chess Records. Actor Adrian Brody starred as Leonard Chess, the founder of the company, while Beyoncé played legendary singer Etta James.

Beyoncé was interested in the role because of James's influence on music. She signed on as coproducer through her own company, Parkwood Entertainment. The company, founded in 2008,

POWER COUPLE

Beyoncé and Jay-Z are powerhouses in both the business and entertainment industries, but they each make their own decisions about their music. "I do my music and he does his music and we respect each other," she said. "We trust we both know what we are doing. If we ever have any questions, I can ask him or he can ask me."[4]

is named after the street Beyoncé lived on while growing up. As a producer, she was involved in all aspects of filmmaking, including the casting and music.

Portraying the tough-talking, heroin-addicted James was an acting challenge for Beyoncé. Beyoncé did a lot of research for the role and studied James's mannerisms. She also visited with women struggling with addiction at Phoenix House, a rehabilitation facility in Brooklyn, New York. "They were so open; I completely admired their courage," she said.[3]

Beyoncé donated her paycheck from *Cadillac Records* to Phoenix House to open the Beyoncé Cosmetology Center, a vocational training center.

Beyoncé portrayed legendary R&B singer Etta James and her struggle with addiction.

Beyoncé and her mother started the facility, which opened March 2010.

MYSTERY WOMAN

James was known to be fiery, bold, and honest in saying whatever was on her mind. Beyoncé said some of those characteristics stayed with her and gave her the courage to try new things with her next album.

People have wondered how Beyoncé is able to give such dynamic onstage performances, when it differs from how she acts in real life. Beyoncé is known to pray before her performances and to be fiercely protective of her privacy. Beyoncé has explained her onstage personality is completely different from her real personality and her onstage outfits are costumes—just part of the performance. "There's my personal life, my sensitive side, and then me as a performer, sexy and energized and fun," she said.[5]

GOING TOO FAR ||||||||||||||||||||||||||||||||||||||||||||||||||||||||||||||||||||

Known to attract a lot of media attention, Beyoncé and Jay-Z have been photographed at awards shows, NBA games, and even aboard their yacht. Beyoncé accepts these intrusions as part of being in the entertainment industry, but one photographer went too far. Beyoncé was shopping for skirts and was surrounded by more than 50 photographers when she left the store. Her bodyguard helped her reach her car, but Beyoncé was shocked when a photographer opened the rear car door, climbed in next to her, and started taking pictures.

Beyoncé had named her onstage personality Sasha. Her 2008 album, *I Am . . . Sasha Fierce*, displayed these dual personalities. One disc is devoted to each personality in the two-disc album. The "Sasha Fierce" disc features the up-tempo songs most of her fans expect, while "I Am" includes more emotional songs that appeal to a broader audience.

Columbia Records began marketing the album on October 7, 2008, by releasing two singles: "If I Were a Boy" from "I Am" and "Single Ladies (Put a Ring on It)" from "Sasha Fierce." "Single Ladies" sold 14 million copies in only one week. The album was released on November 18, 2008, and Beyoncé's film *Cadillac Records* opened two weeks later on December 5.

NO DANCING OFF STAGE

Beyoncé has said she feels awkward whenever one of her songs is played while she's out with friends at a dance club. "Everyone is watching you to see if you're gonna bust a move to your own song," she said.[6] Although she is known for dancing while she performs, Beyoncé refuses to dance when she's not onstage.

Beyoncé uses her performances to show her playful side.

After wrapping *Cadillac Records*, Beyoncé began filming her next film, *Obsessed*, in Los Angeles. She plays the wife of a business executive who is stalked by his female coworker.

Obsessed premiered on April 24, 2009, opening at number one, and it grossed more than $68.3 million in North America. Then Beyoncé left for Zagreb, Croatia, where she kicked off her I Am . . . tour.

Beyoncé performs in Australia
during her I Am . . . tour
in September 2009.

CHAPTER 9

Finding Balance

||||||||||||||||||||||||||||||||||||||||||||||||||||||||||||||||||||||||||||||||||||||||||||||||

Beyoncé had spent months preparing for her I Am . . . tour, which kicked off in April 2009. But even after the tour began, Beyoncé was constantly looking for ways to improve, including staying up late watching recordings of her concert performances and noting what she could do better. "I'm never satisfied," she told a reporter. Then she laughed and added, "I'm sure sometimes it's not easy working for me."[1]

But Beyoncé also remembered what her mother had taught her about finding balance by taking time to have fun. Although she had traveled all over the world touring and promoting her work, she never had time for sightseeing. For this tour, Beyoncé set aside days so she, the band, and the crew could experience the sights in the countries where they performed.

Beyoncé visited churches and museums, admiring architecture all over the world. She also rode a bicycle with others on the tour, discovering how easy it was to ride around without being recognized. Most people did not expect her to be on a bicycle, so by the time they realized it, she had already passed.

REACHING OUT

While performing a September 2009 concert in Sydney, Australia, Beyoncé brought a young leukemia patient named Jada onstage. As she held the girl, Beyoncé knelt on the floor while singing "Halo" to close the show. The opportunity to attend the concert and meet Beyoncé was Jada's request to the Make-A-Wish Foundation. For nine

SHOWING SOME CLASS

At MTV's annual Video Music Awards (VMAs) on September 13, 2009, Beyoncé's video for "Single Ladies (Put a Ring on It)" was nominated for Best Female Video. But singer Taylor Swift won for her single, "You Belong with Me." During her acceptance speech, rapper Kanye West came onstage and interrupted her, saying Beyoncé deserved the award. Swift was visibly shaken, while cameras showed a shocked Beyoncé in the audience. Later in the show, while accepting the award for Best Video, Beyoncé said:

"I remember being 17 years old, up for my first MTV Award with Destiny's Child, and it was one of the most exciting moments of my life, so I would like for Taylor to come out and have her moment."[2]

Amid cheers and a standing ovation, Swift was able to finish her acceptance speech.

years, Beyoncé had been involved with the organization, which grants wishes to children with life-threatening illnesses. It was the fortieth wish Beyoncé had fulfilled.

At another concert, Beyoncé arranged for young women from Girls Educational and Mentoring Services (GEMS) to see her show and visit backstage. Beyoncé became interested in the organization after watching the documentary

Beyoncé won a record six Grammy awards in 2010.

Very Young Girls, a GEMS-produced film about runaways who are sexually exploited. Beyoncé visited the GEMS headquarters in Harlem and decided to get involved by mentoring the girls there and as a spokesperson for the organization's national campaign.

Once again, Beyoncé teamed up with Feeding America on her tour, holding food drives at

some of her concerts. The donations provided
3.5 million meals to local food banks.

A RECORD SETTER

In December 2009, Beyoncé was nominated for
ten Grammy Awards. The Grammy Awards on
January 31, 2010, turned out to be an exciting
night for her. At the show, Beyoncé performed
and took home six awards, including Best Female
Pop Vocal Performance for "Halo" and Song of the
Year for "Single Ladies (Put a Ring on It)." With
her six awards, she set a new record for the most
Grammy wins in a single year by a female. British
singer Adele would tie Beyoncé's record at the
2012 Grammys.

A SURPRISE THANK YOU

At the 2010 Grammy Awards, Beyoncé surprised the audience during her acceptance speech for her final award, saying, "I'd love to thank my family for all of their support, including my husband. I love you."[3] Beyoncé's speech marked the first public acknowledgment and statement of love from the couple, who had been notably quiet about their relationship. When the television cameras panned to Jay-Z, he was clearly surprised.

The I Am . . . tour concluded in February 2010, and Beyoncé decided to take a year-long hiatus, her longest break after 15 years in the business. Even when she had vowed to take time off in the past, her vacations never lasted more than a couple of weeks. But this time, Beyoncé was serious. "I needed some relaxation, but I wanted inspiration too, from regular, everyday things," she said.[4]

Beyoncé spent her free time traveling for pleasure rather than work, playing with her nephew Daniel and picking him up after school, seeing Broadway plays, visiting museums, and sleeping at home in her own bed. Beyoncé went to concerts and enjoyed the experience of being in the audience rather than performing.

Even during her time off, it was impossible to shut down Beyoncé's creativity. So she spent some time learning how to direct and edit videos and also recorded songs for her next album. "I always have to have a project; that's just who I am," Beyoncé explained.[5]

The time off reinvigorated Beyoncé's passion for music and performing. Even though she was

FIRE IN THE KITCHEN

One of Beyoncé's vacation plans was learning how to cook, but unfortunately, there wasn't enough time. She poked fun at her lack of cooking skills in the video for her song "Why Don't You Love Me." She starred as B.B. Homemaker, a 1950s-style housewife. In the video, her dinner catches fire in the oven and she puts out the blaze with a fire extinguisher.

recording during that time, it didn't feel like work at all because it was so natural for her.

Beyoncé had decided to take her time with her fourth album, working on it throughout most of 2010. Some of the music was recorded in studios in New York, and Beyoncé also worked on it while traveling with Jay-Z's tour. She recorded some songs in England and in a makeshift studio built inside a Sydney, Australia, mansion.

Beyoncé performs with virtual duplicates of herself as backup dancers at the *Billboard* Music Awards in 2011.

CHAPTER 10

In Charge of Her Destiny

||||||||||||||||||||||||||||||||||||||||||||||||||||||||||||||||||||||||||||||

Even though Beyoncé co–executive produced her next album, project engineer DJ Swivel said working with her was very collaborative. She listened to everyone's ideas, but ultimately made the final decisions about the music. "If there's something she doesn't like about a track, we're pulling the track apart and fixing it," he said.[1]

THE RIGHT SCENT

Beyoncé has previously been a spokesperson for perfume companies, but in 2010 she released her own signature scent, Heat. It was such a success, Beyoncé introduced two new scents in 2011— Heat Rush and Pulse. Heat Rush is intended to be worn during the daytime and a companion to Heat, which is better suited for nighttime occasions.

It marked the first album Beyoncé did without her father, Mathew, as her manager. In March 2011, she announced he would no longer be her manager, which both Beyoncé and Mathew said was a mutual decision and part of her growth as a performer. "I'm excited about growing," she said. "I've hired my own team of people and started managing myself."[2]

In May, Beyoncé was honored at the *Billboard* Music Awards in Las Vegas, Nevada, receiving the *Billboard* Millennium Award for her achievements and influence in the music industry. Several people paid tribute to her in a video, including Beyoncé's parents, First Lady Michelle Obama, and musicians Lady Gaga, Bono, and Stevie Wonder. Then Beyoncé took the stage for her first-ever performance of her new single "Run the World

(Girls)." Critics and audiences were wowed by the performance, which included Beyoncé onstage with virtual duplicates of herself as backup dancers. *Billboard* staff writers described the performance as "stunning."[3]

NEW RELEASE

Beyoncé's album, simply titled 4, was released on June 28, 2011, only two days after her performance at the Glastonbury Festival in England. It was a mixture of a variety of types of music, including soul, rock, reggae, and contemporary. "I call it my musical gumbo!" Beyoncé said.[4]

In August, Beyoncé promoted the album by performing a series of concerts at New York's Roseland Ballroom. It was an intimate setting with

LUCKY NUMBER 4

Beyoncé's album, *4*, was her fourth one, but she had another reason for choosing it as the title. Beyoncé said four is a significant number for her. Beyoncé and Jay-Z were both born on the fourth day of the month—Beyoncé in September and Jay-Z in December. Also, the couple was married on April 4, the fourth day of the fourth month of the year.

seating for only 3,500 people, much different than performing in a 40,000-seat arena.

BABY BLUE

On August 28, 2011, Beyoncé performed at the MTV VMAs. On the red carpet before the show, she announced she was pregnant with her first child. Then, while performing "Love on Top" from her album 4, she turned to the side, unbuttoned her sequined jacket and rubbed her stomach. Her baby news started a frenzy on the social networking site Twitter and set a new record: 8,868 tweets per second. That beat the previous July 2011 record of 7,196 tweets per second when Japan won the Women's Soccer World Cup.

Beyoncé's daughter, Blue Ivy Carter, was born on January 7, 2012. Two days later, the couple posted the news about her birth on Jay-Z's Web site. A handwritten note accompanied the news: "We welcome you to share in our joy. Thank you for respecting our privacy during this beautiful time in our lives."[5] The note was signed "The Carter Family."

Beyoncé shows off her baby bump during her performance at the MTV VMAs in August 2011.

Over the next few months, Beyoncé spent most of her time out of the public eye and enjoying time at home with her daughter. Then in March 2012, she announced she would be performing a series of three concerts in Atlantic City, New Jersey, during

Blue Ivy Carter became the youngest person to appear on a *Billboard* chart in January 2012. She can be heard crying at the end of Jay-Z's single "Glory," which he released just two days after she was born. The song debuted at Number 74 on *Billboard's* Hot R&B/Hip-Hop Songs chart.

Memorial Day weekend. It was Beyoncé's first performance since the concerts at the Roseland Ballroom in August 2011. And it appeared her fans were very excited to have her back—the concerts sold out so quickly, a fourth day was added.

||||||||||||||||||||||||||||||||||||||||||||||||||||||

LOOKING TO THE FUTURE

By the time she reached age 30, it appeared Beyoncé had done it all as a singer, a songwriter, an actress, a music video director, a producer, a fashion designer, a wife, and a mother. But she has said she has no plans to retire: "The truth is I really love what I do. I live for it."[6]

Beyoncé has plans to continue producing and acting in movies, as well as writing, recording, and performing more music. And she has also

Beyoncé carries daughter Blue Ivy
in February 2012.

EGYPTIAN INSPIRATION

One of Beyoncé's messages in *4* was reminding women they are powerful and can do whatever they want to achieve. A woman who attended one of Beyoncé's concerts served as the inspiration. While performing in Egypt in 2009, Beyoncé noticed a woman wearing a traditional burka sitting on top of a man's shoulders. This surprised Beyoncé, because women wearing burkas are usually not seen on the street after dark in Egypt. Even more amazing was that the woman was waving her arms and Beyoncé could tell that she was singing because she saw the woman's veil moving around her mouth. "Witnessing the power, beauty and strength of women—especially those living in places where their liberties are limited—is what moved me the most," Beyoncé said.[7]

talked about expanding into other areas, including directing and more collaborations with other artists. She'd like to help guide them and teach them what she has learned from being in the music industry.

The thing Beyoncé's most proud of is how her songs have become anthems for young women:

I realize that in those songs I am saying so much of what young women want to say. Whether it is to leave a terrible relationship, working on making themselves better, loving themselves more, or just finding their inner strength, I hear all their stories on the tour and around the world. To have any part in that is amazing.[8]

Beyoncé continues to inspire her fans and be inspired by them. Whatever she decides to do in the future, it will be something she loves. She has said, "I want to make my job a part of my lifestyle so that I always enjoy what I'm doing."[9] Beyoncé hopes to continue encouraging her fans to do the same.

||||||||||

TIMELINE

1981

Beyoncé Giselle Knowles is born in Houston, Texas, on September 4.

1992

Beyoncé appears on *Star Search* as a member of Girl's Tyme.

1996

Beyoncé signs a recording contract with Columbia Records as a member of Destiny's Child.

2001

Destiny's Child's third album, *Survivor,* is released in May and sets a new first-week sales record for a female group.

2001

Beyoncé stars in MTV's *Carmen: A Hip Hopera,* an update of a classic nineteenth-century opera.

2002

Beyoncé appears in her first big screen movie role in July as Foxxy Cleopatra in *Austin Powers in Goldmember.*

1998	1999	2000

Destiny's Child's first album, *Destiny's Child*, is released in February.

Destiny's Child's second album, *The Writing's on the Wall*, is released in July.

Internal conflicts cause members to leave Destiny's Child, which reorganizes as a trio.

2003	2003	2004

Beyoncé appears in her second big screen movie, *The Fighting Temptations*.

Beyoncé releases her first solo album, *Dangerously in Love,* in July and it debuts at Number 1 on the *Billboard* 200.

On February 8, 2004, Beyoncé receives five Grammy awards for *Dangerously in Love*.

TIMELINE

2004

On November 16, Destiny's Child releases its fourth album, *Destiny Fulfilled,* which debuts at Number 2 on the *Billboard* 200.

2005

Destiny's Child announces the Destiny Fulfilled . . . And Loving It tour, its last as a group, and later releases *#1's,* a greatest hits collection.

2006

Beyoncé's second solo album, *B'Day,* is released internationally on September 4, her twenty-fifth birthday.

2008

Beyoncé coproduces and stars as singer Etta James in *Cadillac Records,* which is released in December.

2009

Beyoncé stars in her first nonsinging role in the movie *Obsession,* which opens in April.

2010

In January, Beyoncé wins six Grammy Awards, setting a new record for the most wins in a single year by a female.

2006

Beyoncé stars in *Dreamgirls* and *The Pink Panther*.

2008

Beyoncé and artist Jay-Z are married in a small, private ceremony on April 4.

2008

Beyoncé's third solo album, *I Am . . . Sasha Fierce,* is released on November 18. The song "Single Ladies (Put a Ring on It)" sells 14 million copies in only one week.

2011

Beyoncé's fourth solo album, *4,* is released in June.

2012

Beyoncé and Jay-Z celebrate the birth of their daughter, Blue Ivy Carter, on January 7.

2012

In May, Beyoncé returns to the stage for four concerts in Atlantic City, New Jersey, over Memorial Day weekend.

FULL NAME

Beyoncé Giselle Knowles

DATE OF BIRTH

September 4, 1981

PLACE OF BIRTH

Houston, Texas

MARRIAGE

Jay-Z (Shawn Carter), (April 4, 2008–)

CHILDREN

Blue Ivy Carter

SELECTED ALBUMS

Destiny's Child: *Destiny's Child* (1998), *The Writing's on the Wall* (1999), *Survivor* (2001), *Destiny Fulfilled* (2004)

Solo: *Dangerously in Love* (2003), *B'Day* (2006), *I Am . . . Sasha Fierce* (2008), *4* (2011)

SELECTED FILMS

Austin Powers in Goldmember (2002), *The Fighting Temptations* (2003), *The Pink Panther* (2006), *Dreamgirls* (2006), *Cadillac Records* (2008), *Obsessed* (2009)

SELECTED AWARDS

- Winner of 16 Grammy Awards, three with Destiny's Child and 13 as a solo artist
- Won Best Female Video for "Crazy in Love" at 2003 MTV Video Music Awards
- Won Video of the Year for "Single Ladies (Put a Ring on It)" at the 2006 MTV Video Music Awards
- Won the 2007 *Billboard* Woman of the Year award
- Received the *Billboard* Millennium Award in 2011
- Nominated for 2007 Golden Globe for Best Actress in a Motion Picture–Musical or Comedy for *Dreamgirls* (2006)

PHILANTHROPY

Beyoncé has supported several charitable organizations, including the Make-A-Wish Foundation, Feeding America, and Phoenix House. She and her family have also established the Survivor Foundation, which supports those displaced by natural disasters, the homeless, and people with HIV/AIDS.

"When you are happy, it makes your music better. It makes everything better."

—BEYONCÉ

GLOSSARY

audition—To give a trial performance showcasing personal talent as a musician, singer, dancer, or actor.

chart—A weekly listing of songs or albums in order of popularity or record sales.

choreographer—Someone who creates and arranges the specific movements and steps for a dance.

couture—Highly fashionable and exclusive custom-made clothing.

cowriting—Working with another person to create a work such as a song or album.

debut—A first appearance.

gobsmacking—Something surprising that leaves a person speechless.

Grammy Award—One of several awards the National Academy of Recording Arts and Sciences presents each year to honor musical achievement.

headliner—The main act of a show.

hip-hop—A style of popular music associated with US urban culture that features rap spoken against a background of electronic music or beats.

manager—The person who helps develop an artist's career, including advising the artist on business opportunities and promoting the artist.

platinum—A certification by the Recording Industry Association of America that an album has sold more than a million copies. Multiplatinum indicates that the album has sold more than 2 million copies.

producer—Someone who oversees or provides money for a play, television show, movie, or album.

release—The issuing of a record by the recording company.

rhythm and blues (R&B)—A kind of music that—especially in modern times—typically combines hip hop, soul, and funk.

single—An individual song that is distributed on its own over the radio and other mediums.

soundtrack—The music used in a movie.

studio—A room with electronic recording equipment where music is recorded.

wrapping—Ending the filming of a movie.

ADDITIONAL RESOURCES

SELECTED BIBLIOGRAPHY

Beyoncé. "Eat Play LOVE." *Essence*. July 2011: 111–118. *MasterFILE Premier*. Ebsco. Web. 2 Apr. 2012.

Healy, Mark. "She Is LEGEND." *Marie Claire (US)*. June 2009: 112–117. *MasterFILE Premier*. Ebsco. Web. 27 Mar. 2012.

Smith, Danyel. "Meeting Their Destiny." *Teen People*. Mar. 2001:104. *MasterFILE Premier*. Ebsco. Web. 27 Mar. 2012.

FURTHER READINGS

Cooke, C. W., and Juanmar Studios. *FAME: Beyoncé*. Vancouver, WA: Bluewater Productions, 2011. Print.

Hoblin, Paul. *Jay-Z: Hip-Hop Mogul*. Minneapolis: ABDO Publishing Company, 2012. Print.

WEB SITES

To learn more about Beyoncé, visit ABDO Publishing Company online at **www.abdopublishing.com**. Web sites about Beyoncé are featured on our Book Links page. These links are routinely monitored and updated to provide the most current information available.

PLACES TO VISIT

Roseland Ballroom

239 West 52nd St., New York, NY 10019

212-247-0200

www.roselandballroom.com

Beyoncé performed a series of four concerts here in 2011. Sometimes called The World's Greatest Ballroom, it has featured concerts for over eight decades and continues to offer entertainment for all ages.

SplashTown

21300 I-45 North, Spring, TX 77373

281-355-3300

www.splashtownpark.com

Beyoncé spent her summers going to this waterpark, which is Houston's largest, covering 40 acres.

SOURCE NOTES

CHAPTER 1. AN UNFORGETTABLE NIGHT

1. "Encore: Interview With Beyoncé." *Piers Morgan Tonight.* CNN, 31 Dec. 2011. *Newspaper Source Plus.* Ebsco. Web. 2 Apr. 2012.

2. Alexis Petridis. "Beyoncé at Glastonbury 2011 – Review." *The Guardian.* Guardian News, 26 June 2011. Web. 2 Apr. 2012.

3. "Beyoncé – Single Ladies (Live at Glastonbury 2011)." *YouTube.* YouTube, 27 June 2011. 23 Apr. 2012.

4. "Beyoncé Run the World Girls Glastonbury 2011 HD." *YouTube.* YouTube, 27 June 2011. Web. 26 Apr. 2012.

5. "Beyoncé – Halo @ Glastonbury 2011 HD." *YouTube.* YouTube, 11 July 2011. Web. 23 Apr. 2012.

6. "Encore: Interview With Beyoncé." *Piers Morgan Tonight.* CNN, 31 Dec. 2011. *Newspaper Source Plus.* Ebsco. Web. 2 Apr. 2012.

7. "Beyoncé Chats to Lauren Laverne and Jo Whiley After Her Performance at Glastonbury 2011." *YouTube.* YouTube, 26 June 2011. Web. 2 Apr. 2012.

8. Ibid.

9. Alister Foster. "Camp Sight Beyoncé, Her No 1 Fan . . . And a Trailer for Her 'Risky' Glastonbury Show." *Evening Standard.* 10 June 2011. *Newspaper Source Plus.* Ebsco. Web. 2 Apr. 2012.

CHAPTER 2. A RISING STAR

1. Lynn Norment. "The Untold Story of How Tina & Mathew Knowles Created the Destiny's Child Gold Mine." *Ebony.* Sept. 2001, *MasterFILE Premier.* Ebsco. Web. 27 Mar. 2012.

2. Touré. "A Woman Possessed." *Rolling Stone.* 4 Mar. 2004: 38–44. *MasterFILEPremier.* Ebsco. Web. 27 Mar. 2012.

3. Lynn Norment. "The Soul of Beyoncé." *Ebony.* Apr. 2009: 54–63. *MasterFILE Premier.* Ebsco. Web. 27 Mar. 2012.

4. Lynn Norment. "The Untold Story of How Tina & Mathew Knowles Created the Destiny's Child Gold Mine." *Ebony.* Sept. 2001, *MasterFILE Premier.* Ebsco. Web. 27 Mar. 2012.

CHAPTER 3. A DATE WITH DESTINY

1. Lynn Norment. "The Untold Story of How Tina & Mathew Knowles Created the Destiny's Child Gold Mine." *Ebony.* Sept. 2001, *MasterFILE Premier.* Ebsco. Web. 27 Mar. 2012.

2. Rob Brunner. "Someday We'll Be Together." *Entertainment Weekly.* 1 Sept. 2000: 42. *MasterFILE Premier.* Ebsco. Web. 27 Mar. 2012.

3. "How Gradual Success Helped Beyoncé." *CBSNews.* CBS Interactive, 12 Sept. 2010. Web. 31 July 2012.

4. Charles E. Rogers. "Destiny's Child Makes Impressive 'No, No, No' Debut. *New York Amsterdam News.* 2 Oct. 1997. *MasterFILE Premier.* Ebsco. Web. 27 Mar. 2012.

CHAPTER 4. A ROLLER COASTER YEAR

1. Gil Griffin. "Destiny's Child Expands Creative Role." *Billboard*. 19 June 1999: 20. MasterFILE Premier. Ebsco. Web. 2 May 2012.

2. Beyoncé Knowles, Kelly Rowland, and Michelle Williams. *Soul Survivors: The Official Autobiography of Destiny's Child*. New York: Regan Books, 2002. Print. 90–91.

3. Mark Healy. "She Is LEGEND." *Marie Claire (US)*. June 2009: 112–117. *MasterFILE Premier*. Ebsco. Web. 27 Mar. 2012.

4. John Norris. "Destiny's Child: Then and Now." *MTV Music*. MTV Networks, n.d. Web. 31 July 2012.

5. Charles E. Rogers. "Destiny's Child Still 'Jumping' Up the Charts." *New York Amsterdam News*. 2 Oct. 1999: 23. *MasterFILE Premier*. Ebsco. Web. 2 May 2012.

6. Allison Samuels. "What Beyoncé Wants." *Newsweek*. 29 July 2002: 52. *Academic Search Elite*. Ebsco. Web. 27 Mar. 2012.

7. Rob Brunner. "Someday We'll Be Together." *Entertainment Weekly*. 1 Sept. 2000: 42. *MasterFILE Premier*. Ebsco. Web. 27 Mar. 2012.

8. "Destiny's Child." *People*. 25 Dec. 2000–1 Jan. 2001: 27. *MasterFILE Premier*. Ebsco. Web. 2 May 2012.

CHAPTER 5. SURVIVING

1. Marina Khidekel. "A Date with Destiny." *Cosmo Girl*. Apr. 2001: 110. *MasterFILE Premier*. Ebsco. Web. 2 May 2012.

2. Ibid.

3. Allison Samuels. "What Beyoncé Wants." *Newsweek*. 29 July 2002: 52. *Academic Search Elite*. Ebsco. Web. 27 Mar. 2012.

4. "Destiny's Child: Three the Hard Way." *MTV Music*. MTV Networks, n.d. Web. 31 July 2012.

5. Rashaun Hall. "Destiny's Child Cast as 'Survivor.'" *Billboard*. 5 May 2001: 12. *MasterFILE Premier*. Ebsco. Web. 2 May 2012.

6. Kierna Mayo. "Beyoncé Unwrapped." *Essence*. Aug. 2003: 122. *MasterFILE Premier*. Ebsco. Web. 27 Mar. 2012.

7. Lynn Norment. "Beyoncé Heats Up Hollywood." *Ebony*. July 2002: 36. *MasterFILE Premier*. Ebsco. Web. 27 Mar. 2012.

8. Allison Samuels. "What Beyoncé Wants." *Newsweek*. 29 July 2002: 52. *Academic Search Elite*. Ebsco. Web. 27 Mar. 2012.

9. Jangee Dunn. "Date With Destiny." *Rolling Stone*. 24 May 2001: 52. *MasterFILE Premier*. Ebsco. Web. 27 Mar. 2012.

10. Roger Ebert. "Austin Powers in Goldmember." *Rogerebert.com*. Chicago Sun-Times, 2002. Web. 21 May 2012.

11. Kierna Mayo. "Beyoncé Unwrapped." *Essence*. Aug. 2003: 122. *MasterFILE Premier*. Ebsco. Web. 27 Mar. 2012.

CHAPTER 6. ON HER OWN

1. "Destiny's Child Settles Lawsuits." *AP Online*. 25 July 2002. *Newspaper Source Plus*. Ebsco. Web. 27 Mar. 2012.

2. Touré. "Woman Possessed." *Rolling Stone*. 4 Mar. 2004: 38–44. *MasterFILEPremier*. Ebsco. Web. 27 Mar. 2012.

3. "Picky About Film Roles, Beyoncé Looks to Future." *Washington Times*. 19 Sept. 2003. *Newspaper Source Plus*. Ebsco. Web. 27 Mar. 2012.

4. Lisa Robinson. "Beyoncé." *Vanity Fair.* Nov. 2005: 337–390. *MasterFILE Premier.* Ebsco. Web. 27 Mar. 2012.

5. James Patrick Herman. "Hot Child in the City." *InStyle*. Jan. 2004: 140–147. *MasterFILE Premier*. Ebsco. Web. 27 Mar. 2012.

6. Michelle Tauber. "The Good Life." *People*. Time Inc., 25 Oct. 2004. Web. 31 July 2012.

7. Josh Tyrangiel. "Destiny's Adult," *Time*. 30 June 2003. *MasterFILE Premier*. Ebsco. Web. 27 Mar. 2012.

CHAPTER 7. TOGETHER AGAIN

1. Jeanine Amber. "Beyoncés Destiny." *Essence*. Oct. 2005: 158–165. *MasterFILE Premier*. Ebsco. Web. 27 Mar. 2012.

2. Gail Mitchell. "Beyoncé: Fiercely Creative." *Billboard*. 10 Oct. 2009: 16–22. *MasterFILE Premier*. Ebsco. Web. 27 Mar. 2012.

3. Tamara Conniff. "Beyoncé's Little Secret." *Billboard*. 24 June 2006: 23–23. *MasterFILE Premier*. Ebsco. Web. 27 Mar. 2012.

4. James Patrick Herman. "Beyoncé Reigns Supreme." *InStyle*. Jan. 2007: 59–66. *MasterFILE Premier.* Ebsco. Web. 27 Mar. 2012.

5. "A Whiff of Beyoncé's Hectic Schedule." *USA Today*. 17 Aug. 2007: 14D. *MasterFILEPremier*. Ebsco. Web. 27 Mar. 2012.

CHAPTER 8. NEW CHAPTERS

1. Michelle Tauber. "Beyoncé and Jay-Z Married!" *People*. 21 Apr. 2008: 60–63. *MasterFILEPremier*. Ebsco. Web. 27 Mar. 2012.

2. Jeanine Amber. "I AM LEGEND. (Cover Story)." Essence (Time Inc.) 39.7 (2008): 126. *MasterFILE Premier*. Ebsco. Web. 16 July 2012.

3. Isabel González Whitaker. "Up Close & Personal." *InStyle*. Nov. 2008: 285–295. *MasterFILEPremier*. Ebsco. Web. 27 Mar. 2012.

4. "Beyoncé Brings on the Next Act." *Toronto Star* (Canada). 17 Aug. 2007: L02. *Newspaper Source Plus*. Ebsco. Web. 27 Mar. 2012.

5. Alan Light. "Pop Music's Dreamgirl Awakens Her Earthy Side." *New York Times*. 16 Nov. 2008: 1. *Newspaper Source Plus*. Ebsco. Web. 27 Mar. 2012.

6. Isabel González Whitaker. "Beyoncé's Next Stage." *InStyle*. Sept. 2011: 556–569. *MasterFILEPremier*. Ebsco. Web. 2 Apr. 2012.

CHAPTER 9. FINDING BALANCE

1. Lacey Rose. "Obsessed." *Forbes*. 22 June 2009: 80–89. *MasterFILE Premier*. Ebsco. Web. 27 Mar. 2012.

2. "Beyoncé Gives Taylor Swift Her Moment with a Second Chance." *Starcasm.net*. Chicory Media, 14 Sept. 2009. Web. 11 Sept. 2012.

3. "Beyoncé – 52nd Grammys on CBS: Female Pop Vocal." *YouTube*. 15 May 2012.

4. Beyoncé. "Eat Play LOVE." *Essence*. July 2011: 111–118. *MasterFILE Premier*. Ebsco. 2 Apr. 2012.

5. Isabel González Whitaker. "Beyoncé's Next Stage." *InStyle*. Sept. 2011: 556–569. *MasterFILEPremier*. Ebsco. Web. 2 Apr. 2012.

CHAPTER 10. IN CHARGE OF HER DESTINY

1. Blair Jackson. "Beyoncé Runs Her World: Inside the Recording of 4." *Mix*. Aug. 2011: 54–58. *MasterFILE Premier*. Ebsco. Web. 2 Apr. 2012.

2. Ray Rogers. "The Billboard Q&A: Beyoncé." *Billboard*. 4 June 2011: 22–25. *MasterFILE Premier*. Ebsco. Web. 2 Apr. 2012.

3. "Beyonce Kicks Off Her Own Year-End List." *Billboard*. Billboard, 16 Dec. 2011. Web. 31 July 2012.

4. Isabel González Whitaker. "Beyoncé's Next Stage." *InStyle*. Sept. 2011: 556–569. *MasterFILEPremier*. Ebsco. Web. 2 Apr. 2012.

5. Lauren Effron. "Blue Ivy Carter's First Photos: Beyoncé, Jay-Z's Baby Girl Makes Debut." 10 Feb. 2012. *ABCnews.go.com*. 22 May 2012.

6. Gail Mitchell. "Beyoncé: The Billboard Q&A." *Billboard*. 10 Oct. 2009: 24–30. *MasterFILE Premier*. Ebsco. Web. 27 Mar. 2012.

7. Beyoncé. "Eat Play LOVE." *Essence*. July 2011: 111–118. *MasterFILE Premier*. Ebsco. 2 Apr. 2012.

8. Simon Vozick-Levinson. "Beyoncé's Decade. . . Beyond." *Entertainment Weekly*. 11 Dec, 2009: 38–39. *MasterFILEPremier*. Ebsco. Web. 27 Mar. 2012.

9. Isabel González Whitaker. "Beyoncé's Next Stage." *InStyle*. Sept. 2011: 556–569. *MasterFILEPremier*. Ebsco. Web. 2 Apr. 2012.

INDEX

Austin Powers in Goldmember, 48–51, 53, 55

B'Day (album), 68
"Bills, Bills, Bills," 35, 38, 43
Blige, Mary J., 72
"Bootylicious," 45

Cadillac Records, 72–74, 76, 77
Carmen: A Hip Hopera, 46–48, 49
Carter, Blue Ivy, 90–92
"Check on It," 65
Columbia Records, 28, 29, 31, 33, 35, 45, 76
"Crazy in Love," 9, 56, 57

Dangerously in Love (album), 56, 58–59, 61
Destiny Fulfilled (album), 63
Destiny's Child,
    albums (*see* individual album titles)
    awards, 41, 46
    tours, 40–41, 63–64
Destiny's Child (album), 34
Dreamgirls, 65, 66–67

8 Days of Christmas (album), 48

Fighting Temptations, The, 55–56
4 (album), 11, 89–90, 94
Franklin, Farrah, 38, 40

Girl's Tyme, 19–23, 25–26
Glastonbury Festival, 7–13, 89

"Halo," 11, 80, 83
"Hey Goldmember," 51

I Am . . . Sasha Fierce (album), 76
"If I Were a Boy," 76
"Independent Women (Part 1)," 44

Jay-Z, 56–58, 67, 71–72, 73, 75, 83, 85, 89, 90, 92
Jean, Wyclef, 34

"Killing Time," 33
Knowles, Beyoncé,
    albums (*see* individual album titles)
    awards, 66–67, 81, 83, 88, 90
    business, 65, 88
    childhood, 15–19
    education, 28
    marriage, 71–72
    name, 16

philanthropy, 46, 69, 80–82

tours, 61, 69, 77, 79–80, 84

Knowles, Mathew (father), 15, 16, 18, 20, 22, 26, 27, 28–31, 33, 36–37, 39, 46, 51, 88

Knowles, Solange (sister), 15, 30, 34, 46, 51

Knowles, Tina (mother), 15, 16, 18, 20, 26, 27, 30, 34, 36, 46, 65

Luckett, LeToya, 26, 27, 36–37, 39, 53–54

Meyers, Mike, 48–49

"No, No, No," 34

*O*bsessed, 77

People's Workshop, 18–19

Pink Panther, The, 65

Roberson, LaTavia, 19, 22, 26, 27, 29, 36, 37, 39, 53–54

Roseland Ballroom, 89–90, 92

Ross, Diana, 40, 66, 67

Rowland, Kelly, 19–20, 25, 26, 27, 30, 34, 35, 38, 39, 40, 45–46, 48, 54, 59, 63, 64

"Run the World (Girls)," 11, 88–89

"Say My Name," 10, 37, 39, 41, 43

Silent Partner Productions, 29–30

Simmons, Daryl, 29

"Single Ladies (Put a Ring on It)," 10, 76, 81, 83

Smith, Will, 68

Star Search, 21–23, 25, 26

"Story of Beauty," 45

Suga Mamas, 69

"Survivor," 10, 46, 53–54

Survivor (album), 44–45, 46

Whites, Teresa LaBarbera, 28–29, 31

"Why Don't You Love Me," 85

Williams, Michelle, 38, 40, 45–46, 48, 54, 59, 63

Writing's on the Wall, The (album), 35, 39, 43

ABOUT THE AUTHOR

Barbara Kramer writes biographies for children and young adults. Her books about Ron Howard, Amy Tan, and Alice Walker were selected for the Books for the Teen Age list by the New York Public Library, and her biographies about Mahalia Jackson and Toni Morrison were selected as Notable Social Studies Trade Books for Young People.

PHOTO CREDITS